To Sheila and J.

Christmas 2008

With love from

Jackie & Coli

Easy to see why we love it here!

THE SPIRIT OF THE

DORSET
COAST

ROGER HOLMAN

HALSGROVE

First published in Great Britain in 2007

British Library Cataloguing-in-Publication Data
A CIP record for this title is available from the British Library

ISBN 978 1 84114 576 1

HALSGROVE
Halsgrove House
Ryelands Farm Industrial Estate
Bagley Green, Wellington
Somerset TA21 9PZ
Tel: 01823 653777
Fax: 01823 216796
email: sales@halsgrove.com
website: www.halsgrove.com

Printed and bound by D'Auria Industrie Grafiche Spa, Italy

Introduction

It is not surprising that the Dorset coast is internationally famous for its scenery: there is no other county in southern England that can boast such a variety of landscape, all within 70-odd miles. It ranges from safe sandy beaches, which in the winter months are quite often completely deserted, to towering chalk and limestone cliffs, caves, coves and bays and the unique Chesil Beach, regarded by many as one of the wonders of the world. Then there are the harbours of Lyme Regis, Weymouth, Christchurch and of course Poole, which is the second largest natural harbour in the world, with an indented shore-line of over 100 miles. It is a mecca for yachtsmen and windsurfers and supports a great deal of bird and marine life. In stark contrast is the bleak, windswept Isle of Portland, not pretty but with a definite character of its own.

Because of its unique geology much of the Dorset coast is now considered a World Heritage Site, an honour it shares with such places as the Grand Canyon.

Looking across the Frome to St Mary's church, Wareham.

Opposite page:
Before sunrise is a good time to take a stroll along the beach at Highcliffe.

Boscombe pier and sands with deckchairs awaiting customers.

Opposite page:
Early morning mist on the river at Christchurch.

Sandbanks. A lone fisherman waits patiently for a bite at the harbour entrance.

Opposite page:
Bournemouth Pier at sunset.

Boats in Poole Harbour.

Previous pages:
A wonderful evening afterglow and rising mist in Poole Harbour.

Opposite page:
On the River Frome, Wareham.

Morning frost on Swanage beach.

Opposite page: Handfast Point.

The attractive village of Worth Matravers.

Opposite page: Corfe Castle. Not quite on the coast, but synonymous with the Isle of Purbeck and stunningly photogenic.

Swanage railway.

Opposite page:
Dancing Ledge. Around the turn of the nineteenth century,
the headmaster of a school at Worth
Matravers had this pool blasted out of the
rock so his pupils could bathe safely.

Winspit in calm weather.

Opposite page: St Aldhelm's Head. Sailors treat the turbulent
waters below the Head with the utmost respect.

Emmetts Hill from St Aldhelm's Head.

Opposite page:
St Aldhelm's Head seen from the west.

From Houns-tout looking west.

From Swyre Head looking west.

Clavell's Tower from across the bay,
bathed in evening sunlight.

Opposite page:
Clavell's Tower stands sentinel over Kimmeridge.

During a cold winter, the little stream that trickles over the cliff at Kimmeridge freezes, producing this picturesque effect.

Previous page:
The Kimmeridge Ledges – a favourite haunt of windsurfers when the tide is in – look very benign here, but over the centuries they have caused many shipwrecks.

Distant view of Kimmeridge Bay from above the village.

Bond's Folly, near Creech Grange, donated to the National Trust by J.W.G. Bond, whose family gave their name to the famous street in London.

Opposite page:
Only one or two boats at Kimmeridge are still used to fish for lobsters.

Worbarrow Bay. Claimed by many to be the most picturesque bay in England.

Oposite page: From the promontory of the Tout at Worbarrow Bay the impressive view of Gad Cliff and the coast back to Kimmeridge and beyond can be savoured.

The caves and seclusion of the Mupe area made it attractive to smugglers.

Opposite page:
Looking across Worbarrow Bay to Cockpit Head and Mupe Rocks.

Stair Hole, Lulworth, a miniature Durdle Door created by sea erosion.

Previous pages:
Lulworth Cove. The sea has broken through the hard limestone at the mouth of the bay
and eroded the softer rock behind to form this wonderfully romantic circular cove.

Opposite page: St Oswald's Bay in bright summer sunshine.

Rocks at St Oswald's Bay exposed at low tide.

Evening at Durdle Door.

The magnificent stretch of undulating coast seen looking east from the summit of White Nothe.

Opposite page:
The isolation of Ringstead Bay makes it an ideal place to get away from the crowds.

44

The elegant buildings along Weymouth seafront recall the town's historic royal connections.

Opposite page: Weymouth Harbour.

Weymouth seafront.

Opposite page:
The fine view of Chesil Beach seen from the top of the island at Portland Heights.

Portland lighthouse, synonymous with the Isle of Portland.

Opposite page:
Warm early morning light transforms the
bleak stone houses of Fortuneswell.

Hardy's Monument on Black Down.

Opposite page:
Pulpit Rock.

The swans from Abbotsbury Swannery make their home on
the Fleet, the largest lagoon in Britain.

Opposite page: Abbotsbury and St Catherine's Chapel.

The cliffs at Burton Bradstock.

Opposite page: Chesil Beach, a graveyard for boats since time immemorial.
Thomas Hardy named it 'Dead Man's Bay'.

East Cliff at dusk.

Previous pages: West Bexington, a tiny village right on the beach, is a favourite place for fishermen.

Opposite page: West Bay From East Cliff.

Evening creates a little
magic in Lyme harbour.

Opposite page:
The entrance to West Bay
harbour takes a pounding
during a storm.

Lyme Regis retains an old-world charm, probably because its geography makes expansion impossible.